For

I Do, I Do,

TRADITIONS, POETRY AND IDEAS
ON COURTSHIP AND MARRIAGE

By Esther Budoff Beilenson

Designed by Michel Design

PETER PAUPER PRESS, INC.
WHITE PLAINS · NEW YORK

To my loving husband, Larry

Contents

The Bait

Come live with me, and be my love,
And we will some new pleasures prove
Of golden sands, and crystal brooks,
With silken lines, and silver hooks.

JOHN DONNE

Engagement

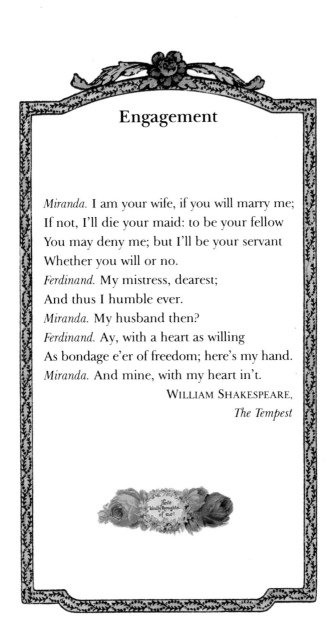

Miranda. I am your wife, if you will marry me;
If not, I'll die your maid: to be your fellow
You may deny me; but I'll be your servant
Whether you will or no.
Ferdinand. My mistress, dearest;
And thus I humble ever.
Miranda. My husband then?
Ferdinand. Ay, with a heart as willing
As bondage e'er of freedom; here's my hand.
Miranda. And mine, with my heart in't.

WILLIAM SHAKESPEARE,
The Tempest

Engagement Rings

The use of rings probably dates back to the beginning of time. During the prehistoric period, primitive man would tie braided grass rings around the ankles and wrists of his bride. It was believed that this act would keep the betrothed's spirits from escaping as well as protect her from any evil spirits lurking nearby.

The Ancient Egyptians wore their engagement rings on the third finger of the left hand, because they thought that the main vein of the heart led directly to that finger.

During medieval times a wedding often served as a social or financial arrangement. The engagement ring functioned as partial payment for the bride as well as a symbol of the groom's honorable intentions. Later on, the engagement ring developed into a more meaningful symbol with the introduction of the gimmal ring. This type of ring was a set of three interlocking rings. The groom, bride, and family friend or witness each wore a part of the ring until the wedding day when all three were united as a single ring for the bride to wear.

In the Nineteenth Century, people began to incorporate jewels and semi-precious stones into engagement rings. "Regard" rings became popular because they used certain stones to spell out endearing sentiments. A common message was "DEAR" using gems such as diamonds, emeralds, amethysts, and rubies. Another favorite message was "LOVE," which combined lapis lazuli, opal, verde antiques, and emeralds.

Today, the diamond solitaire is a very popular choice for many couples. The diamond was chosen for its clarity and value and has come to symbolize enduring love. Interestingly, Princess Di chose a sapphire and the Duchess of York selected a ruby as the stones for their respective engagement rings.

Many brides prefer other stones, however. Here's a list to select from:

For the Bride Who Chooses a Birthstone

January	&#x1F41A;	Garnet or Zircon
February	&#x1F41A;	Amethyst
March	&#x1F41A;	Aquamarine or Bloodstone
April	&#x1F41A;	Diamond
May	&#x1F41A;	Emerald
June	&#x1F41A;	Pearl
July	&#x1F41A;	Ruby
August	&#x1F41A;	Sardonyx or Carnelian
September	&#x1F41A;	Sapphire
October	&#x1F41A;	Opal or Moonstone
November	&#x1F41A;	Topaz
December	&#x1F41A;	Turquoise or Lapis Lazuli

What Birthstones Signify

Garnet		Constancy and Fidelity
Amethyst		Power
Bloodstone		Bravery and Wisdom
Diamond		Purity and Innocence
Emerald		Loyalty and Friendship
Pearl		Good Health and Beauty
Ruby		Nobility and Courage
Sardonyx		Marital Happiness
Sapphire		Truth and Sincerity
Opal		Fearlessness and Consistency
Topaz		Strength and Cheerfulness
Turquoise		Prosperity and Success

It is the woman who chooses the man who will choose her.

PAUL GERALDY

It is always incomprehensible to a man that a woman should ever refuse an offer of marriage.

JANE AUSTEN

Daisy, Daisy, give me your answer, do!
I'm half crazy, all for the love of you!
It won't be a stylish marriage,
I can't afford a carriage,
But you'll look sweet upon the seat
Of a bicycle made for two!

HARRY DACRE

If he proposes marriage to you, it is wisest to accept him immediately, but grant him no undue concessions on the strength of this commitment.

ALEXANDER KING

It was so cold I almost got married.

SHELLEY WINTERS

It is a truth universally acknowledged, that a single man in possession of a good fortune must be in want of a wife.

JANE AUSTEN

The feller that puts off marryin' till he can support a wife ain't very much in love.

KIN HUBBARD

For talk six times with the same single lady, And you may get the wedding dress ready.

LORD BYRON

Never answer a question, other than an offer of marriage, by saying Yes or No.

SUSAN CHITTY

You know, getting engaged just means that we're committed to each other. It's nobody's business when we're getting married. For now, we're just enjoying our lives and having fun.

WINONA RYDER

On the whole, I haven't found men unduly loath to say, "I love you." The real trick is to get them to say, "Will you marry me?"

ILKA CHASE

If you always say "No," you'll never be married.

ENGLISH PROVERB

At the outset I was quite detached. I selected quite objectively from many girls the one who met all the requirements. That girl was Miss Shoda. It later turned to love. I am marrying her because I love her.

CROWN PRINCE AKIHITO OF JAPAN,
the first member of the Japanese royal family to wed a commoner

Marriage

My most brilliant achievement was
my ability to be able to persuade
my wife to marry me.

WINSTON CHURCHILL

Suggested Music for a Wedding

For the Processional

The Bridal Chorus (Here Comes the Bride) from Wagner's *Löhengrin*

Wedding March from Mendelssohn's *A Midsummer Night's Dream*

Fanfare by Couperin

Prince of Denmark's March by Clarke

Sarabande - Suite No. 11 by Handel

Wedding March from Mozart's *Marriage of Figaro*

For the Ceremony

Canon in D Minor by Pachelbel

Ave Maria by Schubert

Jesu, Joy of Man's Desiring by Bach

The Lord's Prayer by Malette

One Hand, One Heart by Bernstein and Sondheim

First Organ Sonata by Mendelssohn

Dodi Li (I am my Beloved's)

Havana Babanof (Beautiful One)

For the Recessional

Fugue in C Minor by Buxtehude

Rondo by Mouret

Benedictus by Simon and Garfunkel

Postlude in G Major by Handel

Ode to Joy from Beethoven's *Ninth Symphony*

Crown Imperial March by Sir William Walton

20

Some Favorite Readings
for the Wedding

Genesis 1:26-28	The Beatitudes (Matthew 5:3-12)
Genesis 2:18, 21-24	Mark 10:6-9
Isaiah 61:10	John 15:9-12, 17:22-24
Hosea 2:19-21	Corinthians 13:1-13
Song of Solomon 8:6	Ephesians 5:1-2, 21-33
The Passionate Shepherd to His Love, by Marlowe	Romans 12:1-2, 9-18
Proverbs 31:10-31	I John 3:18-24
Ruth 1:16-17	Sonnets by Elizabeth Barrett Browning
Ecclesiastes 3:1-9	"Joined for Life" by George Eliot
Selections from Psalms	Sonnets by Shakespeare

From the very first [God] made man and woman to be joined together permanently in marriage; therefore a man is to leave his father and mother, and he and his wife are united so that they are no longer two, but one. And no man may separate what God has joined together.

Mark 10: 6-9
(Living Bible)

Set me as a seal upon thine heart, as a seal upon thine arm: for love is strong as death; jealousy is cruel as the grave: the coals thereof are coals of fire, which hath a most vehement flame.

Song of Solomon 8:6
(KJV)

I will greatly rejoice in the Lord, my soul shall be joyful in my God; for he hath clothed me with the garments of salvation, he hath covered me with the robe of righteousness, as a bridegroom decketh himself with ornaments, and as a bride adorneth herself with her jewels.

Isaiah 61:10
(KJV)

There is a time for everything,
and a season for every activity under
heaven:

a time to be born and a time to die,
a time to plant and a time to uproot,
a time to kill and a time to heal,
a time to tear down and a time to build,
a time to weep and a time to laugh,
a time to mourn and a time to dance,
a time to scatter stones and a time to
gather them,
a time to embrace and a time to refrain,
a time to search and a time to give up,
a time to keep and a time to throw away,
a time to tear and a time to mend,
a time to be silent and a time to speak,
a time to love and a time to hate,
a time for war and a time for peace.

Ecclesiastes 3:1-8

(NIV)

Love is patient and kind; love is not jealous or boastful; it is not arrogant or rude. Love does not insist on its own way; it is not irritable or resentful; it does not rejoice at wrong, but rejoices in the right. Love bears all things, believes all things, hopes all things, endures all things.

Love never ends; . . . So faith, hope, love abide, these three; but the greatest of these is love.

I Corinthians 13:4-8, 13
(RSV)

Hiawatha's Wedding Feast

Sumptuous was the feast Nokomis
Made at Hiawatha's wedding.
All the bowls were made of bass-wood,
White and polished very smoothly,
All the spoons of horn of bison,
Black and polished very smoothly,

She had sent through all the village
Messengers with wands of willow,
As a sign of invitation,
As a token of the feasting;
And the wedding-guests assembled,
Clad in all their richest raiment,
Robes of fur and belts of wampum,
Splendid with their paint and plumage,
Beautiful with beads and tassels.

First they ate the sturgeon, Nahma,
And the pike, the Maskenozha,
Caught and cooked by old Nokomis;
Then on pemican they feasted,
Pemican and buffalo marrow,
Haunch of deer and hump of bison,
Yellow cakes of the Mondamin,
And the wild rice of the river.

But the gracious Hiawatha,
And the lovely Laughing Water,
And the careful old Nokomis,
Tasted not the food before them,
Only waited on the others,
Only served their guests in silence.

HENRY WADSWORTH LONGFELLOW

Wedding Cake

The cutting and sharing of the wedding cake symbolizes the newly married couple's pledge to share their lives together.

This tasty tradition can be traced back to Ancient Rome, where wheat and barley biscuits were broken and sprinkled over the bride's head. The wheat and barley symbolized fertility for the newlyweds, and the crumbs were considered good luck charms by the guests.

During medieval times wedding guests would bring small sweet buns and stack them together. After the ceremony the bride and groom would try to kiss over them, hoping to ensure a long life of love and prosperity. Eventually, a creative baker added the frosting to keep the cakes together and the modern tiered wedding cake was born.

Three-Tiered Wedding Cake

Preparation should begin at least 3 days before the wedding. You will need 3 deep, round cake pans (one 6-inches, one 10-inches, and one 14-inches), 3 foil-covered cake boards (one 6-inch round, one 10-inch round, and one 14-inch round), and 2 tier support sets (one 6-inches and one 10-inches).

Yellow Wedding Cake

(Use recipe that follows to make batter for first set of 3 layers. While layers are baking, use recipe to make additional batter for second set of 3 layers.)

6   *cups cake flour*
4½ *teaspoons baking powder*
2   *teaspoons salt*
2   *cups butter, softened*
4   *cups granulated sugar*
1   *tablespoon vanilla*
8   *eggs*
2   *tablespoons grated lemon or orange peel (optional)*
2   *cups milk*

Preheat oven to 350° F. Grease 3 deep, round cake pans (6-inches, 10-inches, and

14-inches), line bottom of pans with waxed paper, and lightly grease paper. Sift cake flour, baking powder, and salt into large bowl and set aside. Cream butter until fluffy in large mixing bowl of heavy duty mixer. Add sugar and beat until light and fluffy, about 6 minutes. Beat in the vanilla. Add eggs, 1 at a time, beating well after each addition. Fold in lemon peel. Add flour mixture and milk alternately to butter mixture, beating until thoroughly blended.

Spoon batter into pans, filling each pan half full. Place 6-inch and 10-inch pans on upper rack in oven and 14-inch pan on lower rack. Bake 6-inch pan 40 to 45 minutes, 10-inch pan 55 to 60 minutes, and 14-inch pan 70 to 75 minutes, or until cake tester inserted in each cake comes out clean. Cool cakes in pans on wire racks 10 minutes. Invert cakes onto racks, remove pans, peel off lining paper, and cool completely.

Wash and prepare cake pans to use again. Repeat procedure above to make second set of cake layers. When all layers are baked and completely cooled, wrap each layer separately in aluminum foil and store at room temperature until ready to assemble and decorate.

Mocha-Buttercream Filling

¼   *cup butter, softened*
8   *cups confectioners sugar, sifted*
1   *tablespoon powdered instant coffee*
½   *cup unsweetened cocoa powder*
6 to 8 *tablespoons milk*

Cream butter until fluffy. Blend confectioners sugar, coffee, and cocoa powder and beat into butter alternately with milk, beating until filling is smooth and of good spreading consistency. Keep covered until ready to use or cover and refrigerate. Bring back to room temperature before spreading between cake layers.

White Royal Icing
(Prepare 3 separate batches)

1   *cup solid vegetable shortening*
½   *teaspoon salt*
12   *cups confectioners sugar, sifted*
5   *egg whites*
1   *tablespoon colorless vanilla*
4 to 6 *tablespoons light cream or half and half*

Beat shortening in large bowl until smooth and light. Add salt and 6 cups confectioners sugar. Beat until well blended. Beat egg whites until foamy. Beat in remaining 6 cups confectioners sugar alternately with beaten egg whites until well combined. Add vanilla and gradually add cream, beating until icing is smooth and of good spreading consistency. Cover bowl tight and repeat recipe twice. (Icing must be tightly covered at all times. When icing cake, remove small amount of icing and cover remainder while spreading icing on cake.)

To Assemble and Decorate Cake:

Level tops of layers with bread knife or cake leveler and brush off all cake crumbs. Place one 14-inch layer on 14-inch cake board and spread with 3 cups Buttercream Filling. Place second 14-inch layer over filling, bottom side up. Repeat procedure with remaining layers: place 10-inch layer on 10-inch cake board, spread with 2 cups Buttercream Filling, and cover with second 10-inch layer; place 6-inch layer on 6-inch cake board, spread with 1 cup Buttercream Filling and cover with second 6-inch layer. Cover each pair of filled cake layers with thin coat of Royal Icing, smoothing icing with a long, thin icing spatula. Set aside several hours to allow icing to dry completely before applying final coat. Spread thick coat of icing over14-

inch cake and smooth top and sides as completely as possible. Repeat with 10-inch and 6-inch cakes. Set cakes aside until icing is set. If desired, use remaining icing to pipe decorations on sides of cakes.

To assemble cake: Assemble tier supports. Place 14-inch cake on serving plate and insert columns of 10-inch tier support in cake. Spread small amount of icing on top of support to hold 10-inch cake in place. Position 10-inch cake on support and insert 6-inch tier support in 10-inch cake. Spread small amount of icing on top of tier support and position 6-inch cake on support. Decorate cake with fresh flowers, piped icing, and a bride and groom.

Serves about 75.

Champagne Strawberry Punch

2 packages frozen sliced peaches or pineapple chunks
1 lemon, sliced thin
½ package frozen strawberries
1 bottle sauterne
6 ounces brandy
3 bottles chilled champagne

Allow fruit to defrost 2 hours in small bowl, with lemon juices. (Add extra lemon juice if pineapple is used.) Pour over ice, add brandy, and stir. Add chilled champagne just before serving in glasses garnished with peach slice. Makes 42 three-ounce servings.

Champagne Punch

4 ounces lemon juice
4 ounces pineapple juice
3 ounces grenadine or maraschino syrup
3 ounces fruit cordial
8 ounces brandy
1 bottle white wine
2 bottles chilled champagne

Pour all ingredients except champagne over ice, stir, and add champagne just before serving. Garnish bowl with fruit slices. Makes 32 strong three-ounce servings.

Wedding Potpourri

Special occasions such as weddings (anniversaries and births are others) call for the making of potpourri packets or sachets made of ingredients with highly symbolic meanings.

On a wedding day, one may feel a strong attraction to the essence of certain plants, in addition to their beauty and fragrance.

The following recipe should delight the grower, maker, and receiver, especially when used on a special day.

Ingredients for Wedding Potpourri

Plant	Symbolic Meaning
½ cup daisy, white	*Innocence*
1 cup daffodil	*Regard*
½ cup dogwood	*Durability*
¼ cup goat's rue	*Reason*
1 cup grasses	*Utility*
1 cup holly	*Foresight*
1 cup ivy	*Friendship, fidelity*
2 cups mint	*Virtue*
½ cup straw, whole	*Union*
1 cup sweet pea	*Delicate pleasures*

Cut off flowers and leaves of greenery. Let them dry naturally in the air, or microwave them. For individual sachets, use 8″ squares of fabric (or circles about 8″ in diameter). Place ½ cup of the mixed potpourri in the middle, and tie the ball of potpourri with a pretty ribbon. (If you use net or lace instead of fabric, you will be able to see the potpourri.)

The Courtship of Miles Standish

This was the wedding morn of Priscilla the
    Puritan maiden.
Friends were assembled together; the Elder
    and Magistrate also
Graced the scene with their presence, and
    stood like the Law and the Gospel,
One with the sanction of earth, and one with
    the blessing of heaven.
Simple and brief was the wedding, as that of
    Ruth and of Boaz.
Softly the youth and the maiden repeated the
    words of betrothal,
After the Puritan way, and the laudable
    custom of Holland.
Fervently then, and devoutly, the excellent
    Elder of Plymouth
Prayed for the hearth, and the home, that
    were founded that day in affection,
Speaking of life and of death, and imploring
    divine benedictions.
Meanwhile the bridegroom went forth and
    stood with the bride at the doorway,
Breathing the perfumed air of that warm and
    beautiful morning.
Touched with autumnal tints, but lonely and
    sad in the sunshine,

Lay extended before them the land of toil
    and privation;
There were the graves of the dead, and the
    barren waste of the sea-shore,
There the familiar fields, the groves of pine,
    and the meadows;
But to their eyes transfigured, it seemed as
    the Garden of Eden,
Filled with the presence of God, whose voice
    was the sound of the ocean.

Soon was their vision disturbed by the noise
    and stir of departure,
Friends coming forth from the house, and
    impatient of longer delaying,
Each with his plan for the day, and the work
    that was left uncompleted.
Then from a stall near at hand, amid
    exclamations of wonder,
Alden the thoughtful, the careful, so happy,
    so proud of Priscilla,
Brought out his snow-white bull, obeying the
    hands of its master,
Led by a cord that was tied to an iron ring in
    its nostrils,
Covered with crimson cloth, and a cushion
    placed for a saddle.
She should not walk, he said, through the
    dust and heat of the noon-day;

Nay, she should ride like a queen, not plod
   along like a peasant.
Somewhat alarmed at first, but reassured by
   the other,
Placing her hand on the cushion, her foot in
   the hand of her husband,
Gaily, with joyous laugh, Priscilla mounted
   her palfrey.

HENRY WADSWORTH LONGFELLOW

There's a fantasy that you fall in love, get
married and everything will automatically be
all right. But in reality, falling in love is like a
vacation on a Caribbean island. Marriage, on
the other hand, is like scratching a living
from the steep, stony slopes of Sicily. They
are two separate events.

DAVID BIRNEY

It's not beauty but
Fine qualities, my girl, that keep a husband.

EURIPIDES

The secrets of success are a good wife and a steady job. My wife told me.

HOWARD NEMEROV

At the top of the list [of what makes a successful marriage], I think, is a sense of humor. Not feeling competitive, acknow- ledging the other's attributes or whatever it is they do, but not trying to compete with them. And, of course, having a certain outlook on life that is the same, that you want, desire out of life, the same sort of things even if they're expressed in a different way. I think a lot of marriages run into trouble where there's been no meeting of the minds. There's been a meeting of the bods, but not a meeting of the minds. And by that I don't mean you have to be an intellectual genius. But there is something; there's a great deal of understanding.

DEBORAH KERR

A marriage which really works is one which works for others. Marriage has both a private face and a public importance. If we solved all our economic problems and failed to build loving families, it would profit us nothing, because the family is the place where the future is created good and full of love—or deformed. Those who are married live happily ever after the wedding day if they persevere in the real adventure which is the royal task of creating each other and creating a more loving world. That is true of every man and every woman undertaking marriage.

ROBERT RUNCIE,
Archbishop of Canterbury

The best way to hold a man is in your arms.
MAE WEST

People with ungovernable tempers should never marry; people who can't accept reality should never marry; people who don't enjoy responsibility should never marry. In fact, an awful lot of people should never marry.
OLIVIA DE HAVILLAND

Actually, I believe in marriage, having done it three times.

JOAN COLLINS

The main problem in marriage is that, for a man, sex is a hunger—like eating. If a man is hungry and can't get to a fancy French restaurant, he'll go to a hot-dog stand. For a woman, what's important is love and romance.

JOAN FONTAINE

When marrying, one should ask oneself this question: Do you believe that you will be able to converse well with this woman into your old age.

NIETZSCHE

Keep your eyes wide open before marriage, and half-shut afterwards.

BENJAMIN FRANKLIN

Here's to matrimony, the high sea for which no compass has yet been invented.

HEINRICH HEINE

I'll tell you the real secret of how to stay married. Keep the cave clean. They want the cave clean and spotless. Air-conditioned, if possible. Sharpen his spear, and stick it in his hand when he goes out in the morning to spear that bear; and when the bear chases him, console him when he comes home at night, and tell him what a big man he is, and then hide the spear so he doesn't fall over it and stab himself . . .

JEROME CHODOROV AND JOSEPH FIELDS

There has to be, between the male and the female who are going to stay together, some mysterious attraction. And it can't just be sexual. It has to be a respect, an admiration, as women, as men, as *something*.

KATHARINE HEPBURN

By all means marry; if you get a good wife, you'll become happy; if you get a bad one, you'll become a philosopher.

SOCRATES

The perfect mate, despite what "Cosmo-politan" says, does not exist, no matter how many of those tests you take.

SUZANNE BRITT JORDAN

Marriage is a mistake every man should make.

GEORGE JESSEL

Marriage is our last, best chance to grow up.

JOSEPH BARTH

A good marriage is one which allows for change and growth in the individuals and in the way they express their love.

PEARL BUCK

Love

The introduction to this felicity is in private and tender relation of one to one, which is the enchantment of human life; which, like a certain divine rage and enthusiasm, seizes on man at one period and works a revolution in his mind and body; unites him to his race, pledges him to the domestic and civic relations, carries him with new sympathy into nature, enhances the power of the senses, opens the imagination, adds to his character heroic and sacred attributes, establishes marriage and gives permanence to human society.

RALPH WALDO EMERSON

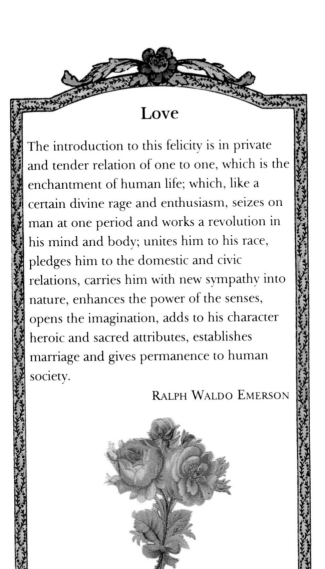

Love Potpourri

Plant	Symbolic Meaning
1 cup heliotrope	*Devotion*
1 cup myrtle	*Love*
½ cup pansy	*Thoughts*
½ cup peach blossom	*I am your captive*
½ cup red clover	*Industry*
1 cup rudbeckia	*Justice*
1 cup sage	*Wisdom, virtue*
½ cup xeranthemum	*Cheerfulness under adversity*

Make sachets as described under "Wedding Potpourri."

If twenty years were to be erased and I were to be presented with the same choice again under the same circumstances I would act precisely as I did then. . . . Perhaps I needed her even more in those searing lonely moments when I—I alone knew in my heart what my decision must be. I have needed her all these 20 years. I love her and need her now. I always will.

DUKE OF WINDSOR,
about his wife

When one loves somebody everything is clear—where to go, what to do—it all takes care of itself and one doesn't have to ask anybody about anything.

MAXIM GORKY

I love thee with a love I seemed to lose
With my lost saints—I love thee with the
  breath,
Smiles, tears, of all my life!—and, if God
  choose,
I shall but love thee better after death.

ELIZABETH BARRETT BROWNING

I learned the real meaning of love. Love is absolute loyalty. People fade, looks fade, but loyalty never fades. You can depend so much on certain people, you can set your watch by them. And that's love, even if it doesn't seem very exciting.

SYLVESTER STALLONE

Romance

I will make you brooches and toys for your
  delight
Of birdsong at morning and starshine at night
I will make a palace fit for you and me
Of green days in forests and blue days at sea.

I will make my kitchen and you shall keep
  your room
Where white flows the river and bright
  blows the broom,
And you shall wash your linen and keep
  your body white
In rainfall at morning and dewfall at night.

And this shall be for music when no one else
  is near,
The fine song for singing, the rare song to
  hear!
That only I remember, that only you admire,
Of the broad road that stretches and the
  roadside fire.

ROBERT LOUIS STEVENSON

Never go to bed mad. Stay up and fight.

PHYLLIS DILLER

Ultimately, I just have to believe and Kevin has to tell me once in a while that ours is the greatest love story. That's kind of what you live on.

CINDY COSTNER

Love requires respect and friendship as well as passion. Because there comes a time when you have to get out of bed.

ERICA JONG

The truth [is] that there is only one terminal dignity—love. And the story of a love is not important—what is important is that one is capable of love. It is perhaps the only glimpse we are permitted of eternity.

HELEN HAYES

Don't you think I was made for you? I feel
like you had me ordered—and I was
delivered to you—to be worn—I want you to
wear me, like a watch-charm or a button
hole bouquet—to the world.

ZELDA FITZGERALD,
letter to F. Scott Fitzgerald

You can see them alongside the shuffleboard
courts in Florida or on the porches of the
old folks' homes up north: an old man with
snow-white hair, a little hard of hearing,
reading the newspaper through a magnifying
glass; an old woman in a shapeless dress, her
knuckles gnarled by arthritis, wearing
sandals to ease her aching arches. They are
holding hands. . . . They are in love, they
have always been in love, although
sometimes they would have denied it. And
because they have been in love they have
survived everything that life could throw at
them, even their own failures.

ERNEST HAVEMANN

Anniversary

Traditional Gifts for Special Anniversaries

First		Paper
Second		Cotton
Third		Leather
Fourth		Fruit
Fifth		Wood
Sixth		Iron, Candy
Seventh		Copper, Wool
Eighth		Pottery, Bronze
Ninth		Pottery, Willow
Tenth		Aluminum, Tin
Fifteenth		Crystal
Twentieth		China
Twenty-fifth		Silver
Thirtieth		Pearls
Thirty-fifth		Coral
Fortieth		Rubies
Forth-fifth		Sapphires
Fiftieth		Gold
Sixtieth		Diamonds

Anniversary Potpourri

Plant	Symbolic Meaning
½ cup campanula	Gratitude
1 cup daffodil	Regard
½ cup dogwood	Durability
1 cup oakleaf geranium	True friendship
1 cup rosemary	Remembrance
½ cup sorrel	Affection
½ cup white clover	Think of me
1 cup zinnia	Thoughts of absent friends

Make sachets as described under "Wedding Potpourri."

There is nothing nobler or more admirable than when two people who see eye to eye keep house as man and wife, confounding their enemies and delighting their friends.

HOMER

Everybody has to be somebody to somebody to be anybody.

MALCOLM S. FORBES

Love is an obsessive delusion that is cured
by marriage.

Dr. Karl Bowman

I've always said that it doesn't matter who
you love or how you love, but *that* you love.
If you're not in love or loving somebody,
you're only half alive. I think it's my most
important message.

Rod McKuen

There is no more lovely, friendly and
charming relationship, communion or
company than a good marriage.

Martin Luther

There are but two objects in marriage, love
or money. If you marry for love, you will
certainly have some very happy days, and
probably many uneasy ones; if you marry
for money, you will have no happy days and
probably no uneasy ones.

Lord Chesterfield

A happy marriage is still the greatest treasure within the gift of fortune.

EDEN PHILLPOTTS

When a divorced man marries a divorced woman, there are four minds in the bed.

TALMUD

Love is being stupid together.

PAUL VALÉRY

There can be only one end to marriage without love, and that is love without marriage.

JOHN CHURTON COLLINS

When a boy lays aside his tops, his marbles,
and his bike in favor of a girl, another girl,
and still another girl, he becomes a youth.
When the youth discards his first girl and his
second girl for *the* girl, he becomes a
bachelor. And when the bachelor can stand
it no longer, he turns into a husband.

ALAN BECK

To love a person means to agree to grow old
with him.

ALBERT CAMUS

I have lived long enough to know that the
evening glow of love has its own riches and
splendour.

BENJAMIN DISRAELI

Grow old along with me!
The best is yet to be,
The last of life, for which the first was made.

MATTHEW ARNOLD

I have performed some marriage ceremonies in my capacity as a judge. I would like to read to you an excerpt from a part of the form of marriage ceremony I prepared: "Marriage is far more than an exchange of vows. It is the foundation of the family, mankind's basic unit of society, the hope of the world and the strength of our country. It is the relationship between ourselves and the generations to follow." That statement represents not only advice to give to the couples who have stood before me, but my view of all families and the importance of families in our lives and in our country.

SANDRA DAY O'CONNOR

I know too many young women today who are desperately searching for themselves, and who have tossed a lot aside to do so. . . . I think you can be a free spirit and still be a giving one, and marriage is one long giving on both sides. I don't think there's enough of that today.

HELEN HAYES

There's nothing worse than solitude,
growing old without a shoulder to lean on.
Marry, marry—even if he's fat and boring.

Gabrielle Chanel

I haven't any formula. I can just say it's been
a very happy experience . . . a successful
marriage I think gets happier as the years go
by, that's about all.

Dwight D. Eisenhower,
on his 43rd wedding anniversary

I sometimes say that 75 per cent of marriage
consists of patience and effort. Love is to
give and take unstintingly . . . I feel sorry for
those who talk about spontaneity and
independence but who ignore patience and
effort.

Nancy Reagan

Shall I Compare Thee

Shall I compare thee to a summer's day?
Thou art more lovely and more temperate:
Rough winds do shake the darling buds of
  May,
And summer's lease hath all too short a date:
Sometimes too hot the eye of heaven shines,
And often is his gold complexion dimmed:
And every fair from fair sometime declines,
By chance, or nature's changing course,
  —untrimmed.
But thy eternal summer shall not fade,
Nor lose possession of that fair thou ow'st,
Nor shall death brag thou wander'st in his
  shade,
When in eternal lines to time thou grow'st;
So long as men can breathe, or eyes can see,
So long lives this, and this gives life to thee.

WILLIAM SHAKESPEARE

Wedding Customs Around the World

AFRICA

Some tribes bind the bride's and groom's wrists together with plaited grass.

CHINA

In China, the color red symbolizes joy and love. Naturally, the bride's dress, candles, gift boxes and money envelopes are often red.

FRANCE

At the wedding reception, the bride and groom drink wine from a two-handled silver cup called the *coupe de mariage*, which is handed down through generations.

GERMANY

During the ceremony, the bride and groom hold candles decorated with ribbons and flowers.

GREECE

Traditionally, the *koumbaros*, a guest of honor who could be the groom's godfather or the best man, will crown the couple during the wedding ceremony and join them in circling the altar three times.

HOLLAND

Prior to the wedding, Dutch families throw a party for the bride and groom. The happy couple receive guests while sitting under a canopy of evergreens symbolizing eternal love.

IRELAND

In Ireland, the customary wedding cake is a rich brandy or bourbon-spiked fruitcake filled with almonds, raisins, cherries and spice. There is always a toast such as, "As you slide down the banister of life, may the splinters never face the wrong way."

ITALY

Traditionally, the newlyweds are showered with sugared almonds, called *confetti*, symbolizing both the bitter and sweet of the life that lies ahead.

JAPAN

The bride and groom become man and wife after the sipping of the first of nine sips of sake.

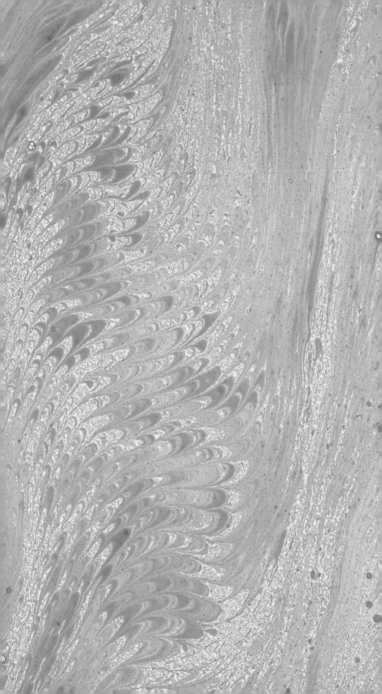